cocktails
STYLE RECIPES

cocktails
STYLE RECIPES

photography DAVID MATHESON

styling GEORGE DOLESE

text NORMAN KOLPAS

executive editor CLAY IDE

A Fireside Book
Published by Simon & Schuster
New York   London   Toronto   Sydney

a toast – to the perfect cocktail

When it comes to entertaining, style is in the details. A well-mixed drink not only makes guests feel welcome, it's also the ultimate way to set the mood for a festive gathering. And like the best parties, the most memorable cocktails are a balance of tradition and originality.

That's why we're pleased to bring you this collection of classic drinks and new variations on old favorites. The recipes have been organized to help you choose the right drinks for any occasion, from an intimate fireside gathering to a backyard barbecue. Throughout, you'll find easy tips and tricks to serve drinks with an extra touch of style that will help you make them – and the event – uniquely your own.

WELDON OWEN

Chief Executive Officer John Owen
President & Chief Operating Officer Terry Newell
Chief Financial Officer Christine E. Munson
Vice President, Publisher Roger Shaw
Vice President, International Sales Stuart Laurence

Creative Director Gaye Allen
Senior Art Director Emma Boys
Project Editor Peter Cieply
Designers Briar Levit, Shadin Saah
Photo Coordinator Meghan Hildebrand
Production Director Chris Hemesath
Production Manager Todd Rechner
Color Manager Teri Bell

Cocktails Style Recipes was conceived and produced by
Weldon Owen Inc.
814 Montgomery Street, San Francisco, CA 94133
in collaboration with Pottery Barn
3250 Van Ness Avenue, San Francisco, CA 94109

Set in Praxis EF™ and Formata™

Color separations by Bright Arts Graphics Singapore (Pte.) Ltd.
Printed in Singapore by Tien Wah Press (Pte.) Ltd.

A WELDON OWEN PRODUCTION

Fireside
A Division of Simon & Schuster, Inc.
1230 Avenue of the Americas
New York, NY 10020

10 9 8 7 6 5 4 3 2 1

Library of Congress Cataloging-in-Publication data is available

ISBN-13: 978-1-4165-7101-8
ISBN-10:   1-4165-7101-9

Photographs: margarita (page 1); kir framboise royale, bellini bella,
berry merry Christmas (from left, page 2); pousse-café (page 5);
choco-mintini (right); dirty martini, vesper, green apple martini,
red vesper (from left, pages 22–23); Manhattan (page 25); frozen
mojito, mojito (pages 48–49); blue Hawaiian (page 51); white
Russian (pages 74–75); cognac and brandy (page 77).

contents

THIS IS YOUR QUICK GUIDE TO **bar** essentials

REDISCOVER ONE OF THE CLASSIC PLEASURES OF ENTERTAINING: SERVING DRINKS FROM YOUR OWN HOME BAR

Hospitality often begins with the simple act of offering guests something to drink when they arrive at your home. No gesture puts people at ease more quickly, providing the pleasure of refreshment and the promise of spirited festivity and lively conversation.

Setting up a bar is easy, whether your home already has one built in or you use a sideboard, counter, cocktail table, or service cart. The following pages outline the basics of preparing your bar, from choosing mixing tools and glassware to selecting accessories and creating garnishes. You don't need a fully stocked bar to prepare most cocktails, however. Make entertaining simple and fun by setting up your bar to serve a smaller selection of drinks, whether our classic cocktails and new twists on old favorites, or your own inspired variations. Your hospitality will be all the more memorable for it.

TAILOR YOUR HOME BAR TO THE STYLE OF THE OCCASION AND THE DRINK MENU THAT YOU'VE CHOSEN FOR IT

When you entertain with drinks, the first step to ensure success is to gear the party to the occasion. Are you hosting casually elegant cocktails before the theater, or throwing a relaxed poolside party? An after-dinner gathering beside the fireplace calls for a different selection of drinks than a barbecue on the patio. With that in mind, we've organized the recipes in this book by the style of occasion to which they're best suited.

Once you've settled on your choices, compile two lists: one with all the ingredients you'll need for the drinks, the other with the mixing tools, accessories, and glassware you'll need to prepare them. Check off the items you already have, and shop in advance for those you still need. Then, before guests arrive, arrange your ingredients and equipment in the bar area, setting them out, as space allows, in a logical and attractive arrangement that suits the order of preparation.

A home wet bar stands ready to prepare an array of classic and contemporary cocktails, from martinis to refreshing blended drinks.

CHOOSING THE RIGHT
GLASSWARE IS EQUAL PARTS
TRADITION AND CREATIVITY

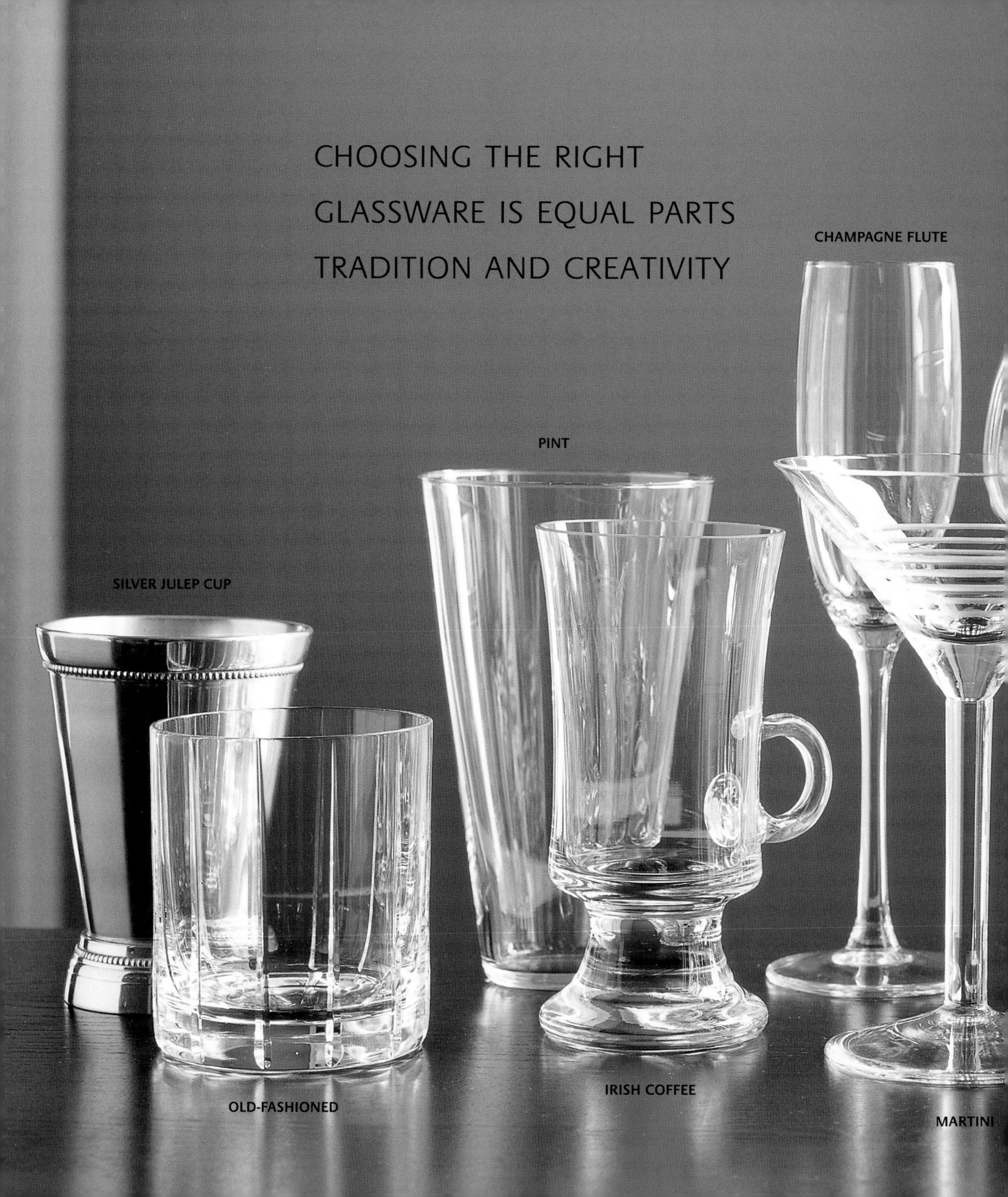

CHAMPAGNE FLUTE

PINT

SILVER JULEP CUP

OLD-FASHIONED

IRISH COFFEE

MARTINI

WINE GLASS

COLLINS

POUSSE-CAFÉ

Never let the lack of a specific glass keep you from making a cocktail. You can always get creative, as long as the glass you choose is generally appropriate for the drink. Long stems let you hold a chilled drink without warming it; sturdy glasses stand up to muddling. Tradition calls for specific glasses to be used for drinks like juleps or old-fashioneds, but don't be afraid to break the rules.

HIGHBALL

MARGARITA

DOUBLE OLD-FASHIONED

BASIC TOOLS FOR PREPARING DRINKS CAN BE AS STYLISH AND BEAUTIFUL AS THEY ARE USEFUL AND FUNCTIONAL

Designed to tailor form to function, the mixing tools you assemble can bring visual style to a home bar. Cocktail shakers feature snug caps with built-in strainers, letting you quickly combine and chill liquids with ice before trickling them into glasses. Mixing glasses and slender bar spoons can be used to stir drinks gently before pouring, and calibrated shot glasses and beakers help you measure potions with precision.

Smaller bar tools fulfill still more specific tasks, including spouts to make pouring from bottles easier; muddlers to crush sugar and seasonings in the bottom of a glass; reamers to extract juice from citrus halves; zesters, peelers, and paring knives to cut garnishes; and scoops or tongs for ice. Many implements may also be found in antique shops, giving you further opportunities to buy tools that are uniquely beautiful.

All the basics: bottle with pouring spout, large and small cocktail shakers, mixing glass, shot glass, and martini pitcher (opposite, clockwise from back); assorted bar tools (left, top); muddler (left, middle); ice bucket and tongs (left, bottom)

ACCESSORIES GIVE YOUR PRESENTATION AN AIR OF OCCASION AND YOUR DRINKS A SENSE OF STYLE

Cocktail accessories serve practical purposes, of course. Coasters and cocktail napkins prevent furniture surfaces from being marred. Small dishes and bowls hold classic complements to many cocktails, like olives or nuts (and an extra bowl provides a place to deposit olive pits). Swizzle sticks let guests re-stir drinks as ice melts. Cocktail picks make it possible to pluck olives and other garnishes from a glass.

Beyond these utilitarian roles, however, your choice of accessories adds to the atmosphere of an occasion. Coasters may be elegant silver, crafted stone, rustic cork, or many other materials. Cocktail picks needn't be standard wood; look for reusable stainless steel ones, or spear olives with playful cocktail umbrellas. There's even the opportunity to create your own original accessories — gluing objects to the ends of swizzle sticks, for example, to make them distinctive.

Cocktail accessories add style: small bowls and reusable picks for garnishes (opposite); swizzle sticks topped with seashells (left, top); a variety of coasters (left, middle); and chocolate-dipped candy cane swizzle sticks (left, bottom).

WHEN HOSTING SPECIAL GATHERINGS, SMALL DETAILS LIKE GARNISHES CAN MAKE A BIG IMPRESSION

Oftentimes, a celery stalk or an olive on a toothpick suffices as a cocktail's finishing touch. With a little additional effort, however, you can achieve eye-catching, casually stylish effects with the drinks that you serve – final flourishes that add both visual appeal and flavor enhancement.

Instead of one piece of fruit, for example, stack thin slices of several kinds with complementary colors and flavors. When fresh cherries are in season, use them instead of bottled maraschino cherries. Look for ideas for unique swizzle sticks like vanilla beans, licorice twists, or beef jerky. Look, too, for ways to vary the ingredients that sometimes coat the rims of glasses, adding flavorful embellishments like chili powder or minced herbs to the salt or crushed candy or grated chocolate to the sugar, to complement a drink's taste and hue.

Garnishes can be simple and still be dramatic: lemon twists and slices give margarita setups fresh appeal (opposite); strawberry and lime slices decorate a blended strawberry margarita (right, top); lemon zests float in champagne cocktails (right, middle); olives and lemon zests are classic martini garnishes.

EASY RECIPES AND STYLISH SERVING IDEAS. WE'LL SHOW YOU

MARYS, AND MANY MORE

classic cocktails

CLASSIC COCKTAILS GIVE GATHERINGS A SENSE OF SOPHISTICATED GAIETY AND ADD GLAMOUR TO ANY SETTING

"Cocktails at six." So begins many a classic dinner invitation, conjuring images of spirited gatherings full of witty conversation and convivial mingling before moving on to "dinner at eight."

The word "cocktail," which originally referred to a mixed-breed horse with a docked tail, was first fancifully used around the beginning of the 19th century to describe mixed drinks that combine one or more spirits, water, sugar, and a dash of bitters — a formula that endures today in drinks like the classic Manhattan (opposite and page 37). Down through the decades, creative bartenders and at-home hosts have broadened that definition to include drinks as varied as the dry martini and its many offspring (pages 26–31), the fruity cosmopolitan family (pages 32–35), and various bloody Marys (pages 44-47). Diverse as they may be, any of these cocktails can help start an evening in style.

martini

ALTHOUGH VODKA OFTEN STARS IN TODAY'S MARTINIS, THE TRUE CLASSIC GETS ITS BRACING TASTE FROM JUNIPER-SCENTED GIN, PLUS A HINT OF DRY VERMOUTH — EVEN IF ONLY A DROP.

serve in style

- Complement the pristine elegance of a classic martini by presenting it on a tray made of silver or other lustrous metal.
- Allow guests to choose their own garnish. In addition to olives stuffed with red pimiento, serve those filled with almond, lemon peel, or onion, or offer whole caperberries. Olives stuffed with anchovies, garlic, or jalapeño chiles provide guests with stronger-flavored alternatives.

1 tablespoon dry vermouth • 3 oz (90 ml) gin • 1 green cocktail olive, for garnish

- Put a martini glass in the freezer, or fill it with ice and water.
- Pour the vermouth into a cocktail shaker or mixing glass; swirl it around to coat the sides of the shaker, then pour it out. (If you prefer a "wetter" martini, leave some of the vermouth in.)
- Fill the cocktail shaker or mixing glass two-thirds full of ice cubes. Pour in the gin. Close the shaker and shake vigorously, or stir in the mixing glass with a bar spoon, for 15–20 seconds.
- Remove the martini glass from the freezer or empty out the ice and water, shaking out any remaining drops. Strain the drink into the chilled glass. Spear the olive on a cocktail pick or toothpick, place it in the glass, and serve immediately.

vesper

1½ oz (45 ml) vodka • 1½ oz (45 ml) gin • 1 oz (30 ml) Lillet Blanc • 1 strip lemon zest, 3 inches (7.5 cm) long

● Chill a martini glass in the freezer, or fill it with ice and water and set it aside to cool.

● Pour the vodka, gin, and Lillet Blanc into a cocktail shaker or mixing glass filled two-thirds with ice. Close and shake the shaker, or stir in the mixing glass with a bar spoon, for 15–20 seconds.

● Remove the martini glass from the freezer, or empty out the ice and water, shaking out any drops. Strain the drink into the chilled glass. Hold the lemon zest strip over the drink and twist its ends in opposite directions to release its oils before dropping it into the glass and serving.

dirty martini

3 oz (90 ml) gin or vodka • 1–2 teaspoons juice from green cocktail olives • 1 teaspoon dry vermouth • 3 green cocktail olives, for garnish

● Chill a martini glass as above. Fill a mixing glass or cocktail shaker two-thirds full of ice. Add the gin or vodka, olive juice, and vermouth. Stir, or close the shaker and shake, for 15–20 seconds.

● Strain the drink into the chilled empty glass. Spear the olives on a cocktail pick or toothpick, place in the glass, and serve immediately.

red vesper

1½ oz (45 ml) vodka • 1½ oz (45 ml) gin • 1 oz (30 ml) Lillet Rouge • 1–3 fresh red raspberries, for garnish

● Chill a martini glass as described at left.

● Follow the instructions for the Vesper at left, substituting Lillet Rouge for the Lillet Blanc in the same proportions.

● Strain the red Vesper into the chilled glass. Spear the raspberries on a cocktail pick, place the pick in the glass, and serve.

martini tips

• The Vesper was James Bond's drink of choice. Look for a paperback copy of Ian Fleming's *Casino Royale*, in which Bond names this martini after his love interest, Vesper Lynd. Photocopy the page on which he orders the drink, and cut the copies for use as tongue-in-cheek coasters.

• For a special presentation, chill a small individual carafe or pitcher along with the martini glass. Mix a double batch of the cocktail, pour the extra into the carafe, and serve it alongside the drink, set into a small bowl of crushed ice to keep it chilled.

• For a modern slant, look for stemless martini glasses that nestle in their own small bowls of crushed ice.

melonball martini

2 oz (60 ml) melon liqueur • 1 oz (30 ml) vanilla vodka • 1 tablespoon lemon juice • 3 balls ripe honeydew melon, cut with a melon baller, for garnish

● Chill a martini glass in the freezer, or fill it with ice and water and set it aside to cool.

● Fill a mixing glass or cocktail shaker about two-thirds full with ice cubes. Pour in the melon liqueur, vanilla vodka, and lemon juice. Stir with a bar spoon in the mixing glass, or cover the shaker and shake it, for 15–20 seconds.

● Remove the martini glass from the freezer, or empty out the ice and water, flicking out any last drops. Strain the drink into the chilled glass. Spear the melon balls on a cocktail pick or toothpick, place the pick in the glass, and serve immediately.

green apple martini

2 oz (60 ml) apple vodka • 1 oz (30 ml) sour apple schnapps • 1 tablespoon bottled sweetened lime juice (such as Rose's) • 3 thin wedges green apple, rubbed with 1 teaspoon lemon juice, for garnish

● Chill a martini glass as above. Fill a mixing glass or cocktail shaker two-thirds full of ice. Pour in the apple vodka, schnapps, and sweetened lime juice. Stir the drink in the mixing glass with a bar spoon, or close the shaker and shake, for 15–20 seconds. Strain the drink into the empty chilled glass.

● Garnish the glass with the apple wedges by spearing them with a cocktail pick or toothpick and fanning them out slightly, halfway down the pick. Place the pick in the drink and serve immediately.

choco-mintini

6 peppermint-stick candies, crushed • 1 tablespoon chocolate shavings • 1 tablespoon light corn syrup • 1 oz (30 ml) vanilla vodka • 2 oz (60 ml) white crème de cacao • 1 oz (30 ml) peppermint schnapps • peppermint sticks dipped in chocolate, for garnish

● Mix the crushed peppermint candies and chocolate shavings, and pour the mixture onto a shallow plate slightly larger than the rim of the martini glass. Pour the corn syrup onto another shallow plate and use it to moisten the martini glass rim; then immediately invert the rim into the crushed candy, turning it until the rim is evenly coated. Chill thoroughly, upright, in the freezer.

● Pour the vanilla vodka, crème de cacao, and peppermint schnapps into a mixing glass or cocktail shaker filled two-thirds full with ice. Stir in the mixing glass with a bar spoon, or close the shaker and shake vigorously, for 15–20 seconds.

● Remove the martini glass from the freezer. Strain the drink into the chilled glass. Insert the chocolate-dipped candy cane, leaning it along the side of the glass. Serve immediately.

cosmopolitan

SINCE ITS RISE TO WIDESPREAD POPULARITY IN THE MID-1990s,
THE "COSMO" HAS BECOME A COCKTAIL STANDARD, WITH ITS
PERFECTLY REFRESHING BALANCE OF TART AND SWEET FLAVORS.

2 oz (60 ml) lemon vodka • 1 oz (30 ml) cranberry juice cocktail •
1 tablespoon Cointreau • 1 tablespoon fresh lime juice • 2 frozen
cranberries and 1 strip lime zest, 3 inches (7.5 cm) long, for garnish

● Chill a cocktail glass in the freezer or by filling it with ice
cubes and cold water and setting it aside to cool.

● Fill a cocktail shaker about two-thirds full with ice cubes. Pour
in the vodka, cranberry juice, Cointreau, and lime juice. Close the
shaker and shake vigorously for 15–20 seconds. (Note: this drink
is best shaken, not stirred in a mixing glass.)

● Remove the glass from the freezer or empty out the ice and
water, shaking out any remaining drops. Strain the liquid into the
chilled glass. Spear two frozen cranberries on a cocktail pick and
loosely wrap with lime zest, and serve alongside or in the drink.

a cosmopolitan approach

● For an elegant and personal
touch, present each individual
cocktail on its own small serving
tray, which can double as a
coaster for the drink.

● For dramatic effect, use a
large tray to carry drinks, still in
their shakers, and glasses to
wherever guests have gathered,
and decant and garnish the
cosmopolitans in front of them.

tropicosmo

2 oz (60 ml) pineapple-flavored vodka • 1½ oz (45 ml) pineapple juice • 1 tablespoon passion fruit–flavored liqueur • 1 tablespoon bottled sweetened lime juice (such as Rose's) • 3 fresh pineapple wedges, for garnish

● Chill a cocktail glass in the freezer or by filling it with ice and cold water and setting it aside to cool.

● Fill a cocktail shaker two-thirds full with ice cubes. Pour in the pineapple-flavored vodka, pineapple juice, passion fruit–flavored liqueur, and sweetened lime juice. Close the shaker and shake vigorously for 15–20 seconds.

● Remove the cocktail glass from the freezer or empty out the ice and water, shaking out any remaining drops. Strain the drink into the chilled glass. Spear the pineapple wedges on a cocktail pick, or cut small holes in them and thread the wedges onto a bendable straw. Serve immediately.

mediterranean

2 oz (60 ml) orange- or mandarin-flavored vodka • 1½ oz (45 ml) bottled pomegranate juice • 1 tablespoon fresh lemon juice • 1 tablespoon limoncello (Italian lemon-flavored liqueur) • 1 strip each lemon and orange zest, 3 inches (7.5 cm) long, for garnish

● Chill a cocktail glass as above. Pour the vodka, pomegranate juice, lemon juice, and limoncello into a cocktail shaker filled two-thirds with ice. Close the shaker and shake for 15–20 seconds.

● Strain the drink into the empty chilled glass. Twist together or tie the lemon and orange zest strips, and garnish the drink by draping the tied zests on the edge of the glass. Serve immediately.

citropolitan

Granulated sugar and grated lemon zest, for coating rim • 1 fresh lemon wedge, for coating rim • 2 oz (60 ml) lemon-flavored vodka • 1 oz (30 ml) triple sec or Cointreau • 1 oz (30 ml) fresh lemon juice • 1 tablespoon bottled sweetened lime juice (such as Rose's) • 1 strip lemon zest, 3 inches (7.5 cm) long, and 1 sour lemon hard candy, for garnish

● Pour a layer of sugar and grated lemon zest onto a plate slightly larger than the rim of a cocktail glass. Moisten the rim of the glass generously with the lemon wedge; then invert the rim into the lemon-sugar mixture, turning it until the rim is evenly coated. Chill, upright, in the freezer.

● Fill a cocktail shaker two-thirds full with ice cubes. Pour in the lemon-flavored vodka, triple sec or Cointreau, and lemon and lime juice. Close the shaker and shake vigorously for 15–20 seconds.

● Remove the cocktail glass from the freezer and strain the drink into the chilled glass. Hold the lemon zest strip over the cocktail and twist in opposite directions to release its oils before dropping it into the drink. Place the sour lemon hard candy in the glass and serve immediately.

manhattan

2½ oz (75 ml) whiskey (preferably bourbon or rye) • 1½ tablespoons sweet vermouth • 2 dashes Angostura bitters • 1 small strip fresh orange peel • 1 maraschino cherry with stem, for garnish

● Chill a cocktail glass in the freezer.

● Fill a cocktail shaker two-thirds full with ice cubes. Pour in the whiskey and sweet vermouth; add the bitters. Close the shaker and shake vigorously for 15–20 seconds. Strain the drink into the chilled glass. Twist the orange peel between your fingers to release its oils, and rub the orange part around the rim of the glass; discard the peel. Garnish with the cherry and serve.

metropolitan flair

● Add a sense of club-room sophistication by presenting the Manhattan to your guest on a leather coaster.

● To spark conversation, pick up copies of your favorite New York City newspaper and leave them folded on the cocktail table.

SOME COCKTAILS JUST CAN'T BE IMPROVED UPON. THE MANHATTAN HAS BEEN A CLASSIC SINCE THE LATE 19TH CENTURY, AND THOUGH SOURS MAY BE MADE WITH OTHER LIQUORS, WHISKEY IS THE DEFINITIVE CHOICE.

whisky sour

2 ounces (60 ml) Canadian blended whisky • 1½ tablespoons fresh lemon juice • 1½ teaspoons superfine sugar • 1 thin slice fresh orange, seeded, for garnish • 1 maraschino cherry with stem, for garnish

● Chill a sour glass or other cocktail glass in the freezer.

● Fill a cocktail shaker two-thirds full with ice cubes. Pour in the whisky and lemon juice and add the sugar. Close the shaker and shake vigorously for 15–20 seconds.

● Remove the sour glass from the freezer. Strain the drink into the chilled glass. Twist the orange slice to release some of its juice, and add it and the cherry to the glass. Serve immediately.

sour garnishes

● Use a cocktail pick to skewer the orange slice and cherry together, for easier removal.

● For a more exotic effect, in place of the orange and cherry, substitute a whole fresh kumquat on a toothpick or cocktail stick; kumquats are edible, peel and all.

tom collins

2 oz (60 ml) gin • 1 oz (30 ml) fresh lemon juice • 2 teaspoons superfine sugar • 4–6 oz (120–180 ml) club soda • 1 orange wedge and 1 maraschino cherry, for garnish

- Fill a cocktail shaker two-thirds full with ice cubes. Add the gin, lemon juice, and sugar. Close the cocktail shaker and shake vigorously for 15–20 seconds.

- Fill a Collins glass with ice cubes. Strain the cocktail into the glass. Pour in the club soda to taste, and stir briefly with a swizzle stick. Garnish with the orange wedge, squeezing it slightly, and the cherry. Serve immediately.

tall and cool

- For the traditional presentation, use one of the tall, narrow, straight-sided glasses specifically known as a "Collins glass."
- A Collins simply doesn't seem complete without a swizzle stick. Clear sticks are classic, but many options are available.

LEGEND HAS IT THAT THE LEMON-SCENTED TOM COLLINS WAS INVENTED IN LONDON AND NAMED FOR THE BARTENDER WHO CREATED IT, AND THE SIDECAR IN PARIS, TO WARM A MOTORCYCLING WWI CAPTAIN.

sidecar

granulated sugar and 1 lemon wedge, for coating rim • 2 oz (60 ml) brandy • 1 oz (30 ml) triple sec • 1 oz (30 ml) fresh lemon juice

- Pour a layer of sugar onto a plate slightly larger than the rim of a cocktail glass. Squeezing the lemon wedge between your fingers, use it to moisten the rim of the glass generously; then immediately invert the rim into the granulated sugar, turning it until the rim is evenly coated. Chill thoroughly, upright, in the freezer.

- Fill a cocktail shaker two-thirds full with ice. Add the brandy, triple sec, and lemon juice. Cover and shake for 15–20 seconds. Strain the cocktail into the glass and serve.

creative color

- For a more colorful rim coating, mix the granulated sugar with some finely grated lemon zest.
- After moistening the glass's rim with lemon juice, coat only half of it with sugar or sugar and lemon zest, giving your guest the option of sweet or tangy sips.

mint julep

THE SIGNATURE DRINK OF THE KENTUCKY DERBY IS TRADITIONALLY
SERVED IN A SILVER JULEP CUP, THE EXTERIOR OF WHICH DEVELOPS
AN ENTICING LAYER OF FROST WHEN THE COCKTAIL IS MIXED.

derby chic

- Wrap a silver julep cup for decorative effect. Use a wide grosgrain ribbon to tie a bow, or double it to form a "ribbon cozy" that protects hands from the cold surface of the cup. Using a ribbon with wire reinforcement allows you to create a decorative bow that will retain its shape.

- Stylish stainless-steel or other metal cups are also available.

1 or 2 sugar cubes • 4 large fresh mint leaves • 3 oz (90 ml) bourbon • 3 large mint sprigs, for garnish

- Put 1 or 2 sugar cubes and the mint leaves in the bottom of a silver julep cup or a highball or old-fashioned glass. With a muddler, muddle the sugar cubes and mint, crushing them together until the mint leaves are fragrant.

- Fill the julep cup or the glass with crushed ice.

- Pour in the bourbon. Stir well with a bar spoon or a swizzle stick to thoroughly combine the sugar, mint, and bourbon; if using a julep cup, stir until a thin film of frost forms on the outside. Garnish with mint sprigs, crushing them slightly before setting them atop the drink, and serve immediately.

cozy julep

4 large sprigs fresh mint • 1 sugar cube • 3 oz (90 ml) Southern Comfort • 1 lemon slice, for garnish

● Put three mint sprigs and the sugar cube in the bottom of a julep cup or a highball or double old-fashioned glass. With a muddler, firmly but gently pound and grind the mint sprigs and sugar together until the mint is partially crushed.

● Fill the cup or glass with crushed ice. Pour in the Southern Comfort and stir well with a bar spoon or swizzle stick; if using a julep cup, stir until a film of frost forms on the outside. Garnish with the lemon slice and remaining mint sprig and serve.

sparkling lemonade julep

1 large sprig fresh mint • 1 tablespoon superfine sugar • 2 oz (60 ml) lemon juice • 1½ oz (45 ml) bourbon • 4 oz (120 ml) club soda • 1 slice lemon, seeded, for garnish

● In the bottom of a sturdy highball glass, firmly but gently pound and grind the mint sprig, sugar, and lemon juice with a muddler until the sugar is dissolved. Stir in the bourbon.

● Fill the glass loosely with ice cubes. Pour in the club soda. Stir well with a bar spoon. Garnish with the lemon slice on top, or, cut a slit in the slice from the center to the edge halfway across, slip it onto the edge of the glass, and serve.

peach julep

3 large sprigs fresh mint • 3 oz (90 ml) peach brandy • 2 drops Angostura bitters • 1 wedge ripe fresh peach, for garnish

● Place the mint sprigs in the bottom of a julep cup or a highball or old-fashioned glass. With a muddler, firmly but gently pound the mint sprigs until they are partially crushed and aromatic.

● Fill the cup or glass with ice. Add the peach brandy and bitters and stir with a bar spoon for 15–20 seconds or, if using a julep cup, until a film of frost forms on the outside. Garnish with the peach slice, placing it on top of the ice, and serve.

southern style

● Add a touch of the Old South by placing a glossy magnolia leaf or other large plant leaf beneath each drink.

● For a more minty-tasting julep, steep the fresh herbs in the spirit for several hours before mixing.

● Make a mint simple syrup for use in juleps or other drinks. Simmer together a bunch of cleaned mint leaves (about 1½ oz/45 g), 1 cup of sugar (250 g), and 2 cups of water (500 ml) in a small saucepan for about five minutes. Before use, cool and remove mint.

bloody mary

AN AMERICAN FAVORITE, THIS DRINK WAS INVENTED AT HARRY'S NEW YORK BAR IN PARIS IN THE 1920s. MANY BARTENDERS HAVE SIGNATURE WAYS TO ADD AN EXTRA JOLT, SUCH AS THE GRATED HORSERADISH IN THIS RECIPE.

extra zing

● Add excitement to the flavor and appearance by sprinkling freshly ground pepper (shown above) or fresh chiles into the ice cube tray before freezing cubes.

● Coat the rims of the glasses by moistening them with fresh lime juice and rolling them in a mixture of salt and mild or medium-hot chili powder.

2 oz (60 ml) vodka • 4 oz (120 ml) high-quality canned or bottled tomato juice • 1½ tablespoons fresh lime juice • ¼ teaspoon prepared horseradish • ¼ teaspoon Worcestershire sauce • ¼ teaspoon hot pepper sauce (such as Tabasco) • ¼ teaspoon freshly ground black pepper • ⅛ teaspoon celery salt • 1 celery stalk, for garnish

● Fill a cocktail shaker two-thirds full with ice cubes. Add the vodka, tomato juice, lime juice, horseradish, Worcestershire sauce, hot pepper sauce, black pepper, and celery salt.

● Cover the cocktail shaker and shake for 15–20 seconds. Place the celery stalk in a pint or double old-fashioned glass and fill it with ice cubes. Strain the cocktail into the glass and serve.

● The spiciness of this cocktail is easy to control. For a hotter drink, use pepper-flavored vodka or more hot pepper sauce; for more zing but a gentler heat, increase the amount of horseradish.

blushing mary

1 cup (250 ml) high-quality canned or bottled tomato juice • 1½ oz (45 ml) hot chili pepper vodka • 1 oz (30 ml) fresh lime juice • ¼ teaspoon Worcestershire sauce • ⅛ teaspoon freshly ground white pepper • ⅛ teaspoon salt • ½ lime slice and 1 cherry tomato, for garnish

● An hour before serving time, line a fine-mesh sieve or a large, clean coffee-filter cone with a paper coffee filter, and set it over a mixing glass. Pour the tomato juice into the filter and let it drain until all that remains is a thick paste of tomato solids. There should be about 5 oz (150 ml) of translucent red tomato "water" in the glass. (If you're planning to serve several drinks, adjust the amount of juice that you filter accordingly.)

● Chill a martini glass in the freezer or by filling it with ice and cold water and setting it aside.

● Fill a cocktail shaker two-thirds full with ice cubes. Add 4 oz (120 ml) of the tomato water, along with the pepper vodka, lime juice, Worcestershire sauce, white pepper, and salt. Cover and shake vigorously for 15–20 seconds.

● Remove the martini glass from the freezer, or empty out the ice and water, shaking out any remaining drops. Strain the drink into the glass. With a cocktail pick, spear the lime slice and the tomato, and place the garnish in the drink, leaning it against the rim of the glass. Serve immediately.

bloody bull

2 oz (60 ml) vodka • 3 oz (90 ml) canned beef broth • 2 oz (60 ml) high-quality canned or bottled tomato juice • 1 tablespoon fresh lemon juice • ¼ teaspoon Worcestershire sauce • ⅛ teaspoon hot pepper sauce (such as Tabasco) • ⅛ teaspoon freshly ground black pepper • ⅛ teaspoon celery salt • 1 lemon wedge, for garnish • 1 stick beef jerky, for garnish (optional)

● Fill a cocktail shaker two-thirds full with ice cubes. Add the vodka, beef broth, tomato juice, lemon juice, Worcestershire sauce, hot pepper sauce, black pepper, and celery salt.

● Shake for 15–20 seconds. Fill an iced tea or pint glass with ice cubes. Strain the cocktail into the glass. Garnish with the lemon wedge and, if you like, the beef jerky. Serve immediately.

michelada

6 oz (180 ml) lager-style Mexican beer (such as Corona or Pacifico) • ½ fresh lime • hot pepper sauce (such as Tabasco) • 4 oz (120 ml) high-quality canned or bottled tomato juice • ⅛ teaspoon salt

● Fill a large iced tea or pint glass with ice cubes. Slowly pour in the beer. When the foam subsides, squeeze in the lime, dropping it into the glass, and add several drops of hot pepper sauce to taste.

● Slowly pour in the tomato juice. Add the salt and stir briefly and gently with a swizzle stick or bar spoon before serving.

SATISFIES THIRST LIKE DRINKS THAT BEGIN WITH ICE AND SPIRITS,

TO CREATE PERFECT quenching refreshers

NO MATTER WHAT THIRST-QUENCHING REFRESHER YOU PLAN TO SERVE, ONE INGREDIENT IS ESSENTIAL: LOTS OF ICE

"Breaking the ice" is a perfect metaphor for getting a party rolling. Not only does it evoke images of clear sailing ahead but, especially when the weather is hot, it also holds out the hope of well-chilled drinks.

Always keep plenty of ice on hand when you plan to serve any of the drinks in this chapter. Some, such as margaritas (pages 52–55) and the blue Hawaiian (opposite and page 57), are most commonly served on the rocks. Blended drinks require a generous amount of ice per serving to produce a thick, shiver-inducing slush; and champagne or sparkling wine used for champagne cocktails (pages 70–73) is quickly and effectively chilled in a bucket filled with ice. So check your freezer's ice maker to see that it's turned on and filled to capacity, and be prepared to supplement your supply with a trip to the market.

margarita

SINCE AT LEAST THE 1940s, MARGARITAS AND PARTIES HAVE BEEN INSEPARABLE, ESPECIALLY AT POOLSIDE OR PATIO GATHERINGS. THE SWEET-CITRUS MIX IS A COOL FOIL FOR THE WARMTH OF TEQUILA.

coarse salt and 1 lime wedge, for coating rim (optional) • 2 oz (60 ml) tequila (use a top-shelf brand for best taste) • 1½ oz (45 ml) Cointreau or Grand Marnier • 1 oz (30 ml) fresh lime juice • 1 slice lime, for garnish

- Pour a shallow layer of salt onto a plate slightly larger than the rim of a cocktail or old-fashioned glass. Lightly squeeze the lime wedge and use it to moisten the rim of the glass. Invert the glass into the salt to coat the rim. Using a scoop or tongs, fill the glass with ice cubes, taking care not to disturb the salt rim.

- Fill a cocktail shaker two-thirds full with ice cubes. Add the tequila, Cointreau or Grand Marnier, and lime juice. Cover and shake vigorously for 15–20 seconds. Strain the cocktail into the ice-filled, salt-rimmed glass and serve immediately. As with many cocktails, margaritas may also be served "up." Simply strain the drink into a chilled martini glass and garnish with lime.

summer splash

- Instead of using coasters, look for glasses that fit into their own basket-weave holders that also keep hands from feeling chilled.
- Garnish the cocktails with a decorative lime "pinwheel." Cut a thin slice of lime, then make a slit halfway across its diameter, from the center to one side. Pass a cocktail umbrella or pick through one corner, then twist the other corner down and pass the pick through it.

blended mango margarita

coarse salt and 1 lime wedge, for coating rim (optional) • 2 oz (60 ml) tequila • 1 oz (30 ml) bottled sweetened lime juice (such as Rose's) • 1 medium ripe mango, peeled, flesh cut from pit, and 3 thin wedges saved for garnish • 1 cup (250 ml) ice cubes

● If you enjoy a salt-crusted rim, pour a shallow layer of salt onto a plate slightly larger than the rim of a margarita or old-fashioned glass. Lightly squeeze the lime wedge and moisten the rim of the glass with it. Invert the glass into the salt to coat the rim. Put the glass in the freezer to chill.

● Put the tequila, sweetened lime juice, mango flesh, and ice cubes into the jar of a bar blender. Cover and blend until smooth, about 30 seconds.

● Pour the cocktail into the chilled glass. Spear the mango wedges on a cocktail pick and place it in the glass, leaning it against the rim, and serve.

flavor twists

● Many fruits work well for margaritas. Besides the ones here, possibilities include banana, blueberry, cranberry, papaya, passion fruit, peach, pineapple, and raspberry.

● For a more complex flavor, use a *reposado* (briefly aged) or *añejo* (aged for a year or more) tequila.

blended strawberry margarita

2 oz (60 ml) tequila • 1 oz (30 ml) bottled sweetened lime juice • 1 cup (250 ml) fresh or frozen strawberries • 1 cup (250 ml) ice cubes • 2–3 teaspoons superfine sugar • fresh strawberry and lime slices, for garnish

● Place a margarita glass in the freezer to chill. If you like a salt-crusted rim, follow the instructions at left before chilling the glass.

● Combine the tequila, sweetened lime juice, strawberries, ice cubes, and sugar in the blender. Cover and blend for about 30 seconds.

● Pour the cocktail into the chilled glass. With a cocktail pick, spear three strawberry slices, with two small lime slices alternated between them, and garnish the drink. Serve immediately.

blended citrus margarita

2 oz (60 ml) tequila • 1½ oz (45 ml) triple sec or Cointreau • 1 tablespoon fresh lemon juice • 1 tablespoon fresh lime juice • 1 cup (250 ml) ice cubes • 1 each lemon, lime, and orange slice, for garnish

● Chill a margarita or cocktail glass and salt the rim if desired. Blend the tequila, triple sec or Cointreau, lemon and lime juice, and ice in a blender, as above, for about 30 seconds. Pour the drink into the chilled glass. Slightly fold and then spear the three citrus slices with a cocktail pick and lay the garnish across the top of the glass.

mai tai

1 oz (30 ml) golden rum • 1 oz (30 ml) white rum • 1 oz (30 ml) triple sec • 1 oz (30 ml) fresh lime juice • 1 oz (30 ml) orgeat syrup (see Glossary, page 93) • 1½ teaspoons superfine sugar • 1 oz (30 ml) dark rum • 1 maraschino cherry and one sprig fresh mint, for garnish

• Fill a cocktail shaker two-thirds full with ice cubes. Add the golden and white rum, triple sec, lime juice, orgeat, and sugar. Cover and shake for 15–20 seconds.

• Fill a double old-fashioned glass nearly full with crushed ice. Strain the drink into the glass. Pour the dark rum in, floating it on the surface. Garnish with the cherry and mint sprig, and serve.

perfect pairings

• Make a frozen mai tai by blending all the ingredients except the dark rum together with one cup of ice, then float the dark rum on top.

• Serve a bowl of almonds alongside the drink, to pick up the flavor of the orgeat syrup.

ORIGINALLY CREATED AT TRADER VIC'S RESTAURANT, THE MAI TAI IS A TROPICAL CLASSIC THAT STILL PACKS A PUNCH. THE BLUE HAWAIIAN'S AZURE COLOR CONJURES THE WATERS OF ITS NAMESAKE ISLANDS.

blue hawaiian

1 oz (30 ml) light rum • 1 oz (30 ml) blue curaçao • 2 oz (60 ml) pineapple juice • 1 tablespoon superfine sugar • 1 tablespoon lemon juice • 1 tablespoon fresh lime juice • 1 oz (30 ml) cream of coconut (optional) • 1 maraschino cherry and 1 pineapple wedge, for garnish

• Put the light rum, blue curaçao, pineapple juice, sugar, lemon and lime juice, and cream of coconut (if using) into a cocktail shaker filled two-thirds full of ice, and shake for 15–20 seconds.

• Fill a tall highball or Collins glass with ice cubes. Strain the cocktail into the glass. Garnish with the maraschino cherry and and pineapple wedge, and serve immediately.

tropical touches

• You can create decorative wraps for drinks that not only enhance their presentation but also make cold drinks more comfortable to hold. Here, a coconut bark strip is tied with natural raffia and a ti plant leaf is tied with green raffia.

sangria

SPAIN'S FAMED RED-WINE PUNCH GETS ITS PLEASANT SWEETNESS
FROM FRESH FRUIT AND A TOUCH OF SUGAR. SPLASHES OF BRANDY
AND ORANGE-FLAVORED LIQUEUR ADD A DISARMING KICK.

2 oz (60 ml) brandy • 2 oz (60 ml) orange-flavored liqueur (such
as Cointreau or Grand Marnier) • 4 tablespoons superfine sugar •
1 (750-ml) bottle dry red wine, preferably Spanish • 1 cup (250 ml)
orange juice • 1 oz (30 ml) lemon juice • 1 orange, thinly sliced and
seeded • 1 lemon, thinly sliced and seeded • 2 cups (500 ml) club soda

● In a large nonreactive punch bowl or pitcher (made of a
material that does not react to acids, such as glass, stainless steel,
or enameled metal), stir together the brandy, orange liqueur, and
sugar until the sugar dissolves. Stir in the wine, orange juice,
lemon juice, and fruit slices. Though the sangria may be served
right away, it's better to cover and refrigerate it for 2–4 hours.

● Just before serving, pour in the club soda and stir briefly. Fill
old-fashioned, highball, or wine glasses with ice cubes. Pour or
ladle the sangria, with the fruit slices, into the glasses and serve.

fresh tips

● Hand-painted tiles from Spain
or Mexico make perfect coasters
for this Latin libation.

● Many drinks use citrus slices
as a garnish. A simple way to
make them more stylish is to fold
two or more slices together, then
spear them on a cocktail pick.

● If you don't have a punch
bowl to mix the sangria, try using
a large, sturdy hurricane lantern
or vase instead.

one To offer a choice of sangrias, assemble ingredients from several recipes (see pages 59 and 63): red and white wines, fresh fruit, spirits, juices, sparkling beverages, and sugar.

two Mix the sangrias in separate containers, following the recipes. Depending upon the size and length of the party, keep extra ingredients on hand to replenish each sangria.

three Before serving, label
each choice of sangria by tying a
ribbon with an identifying tag around
the punch bowl or pitcher. Assemble
glasses and coasters.

four Make extra fruit garnishes
by spearing fruit slices on cocktail
picks. Before serving, stir the soda
into the sangria. Fill the glasses with
ice, ladle in the sangria, and garnish.

fruity sangria blanca

4 oz (120 ml) Cointreau or triple sec • 2 tablespoons superfine sugar • 1 (750-ml) bottle dry white wine, preferably Spanish • ½ cup (125 ml) fresh orange juice • 1 oz (30 ml) lemon juice • 2 ripe peaches, halved, pitted, and thinly sliced • 2 ripe plums, halved, pitted, and thinly sliced • 1 lemon, thinly sliced and seeded • ½ pound (250 g) fresh cherries, pitted • 1¾ cups (355 ml) lemon-lime soda

• In a large nonreactive pitcher or punch bowl (glass, stainless steel, or enameled metal), stir together the Cointreau or triple sec and sugar until the sugar dissolves. Stir in the wine, orange juice, lemon juice, and fruit slices. Hold each cherry over the pitcher or bowl, squeeze gently to release some of its juice, and drop it into the liquid. If time allows, cover and refrigerate the sangria for 2–4 hours, although you may serve it right away.

• Just before serving, stir in the lemon-lime soda. Fill glasses with ice cubes. Ladle the sangria, with the fruit slices, into the glasses and serve.

tropical sangria mexicana

2 oz (60 ml) tequila • 2 oz (60 ml) triple sec or Cointreau • 6 tablespoons superfine sugar • 1 (750-ml) bottle dry red wine • 1 cup (250 ml) pineapple juice • 2 oz (60 ml) fresh lime juice • 1 small, ripe pineapple, peeled, cored, and sliced into rings • 1 small ripe mango, peeled, pitted, and cubed • 2 limes, thinly sliced and seeded • 2 cups (500 ml) club soda

• In a large nonreactive pitcher or punch bowl, stir together the tequila, triple sec or Cointreau, and sugar until the sugar dissolves. Stir in the wine, pineapple juice, lime juice, pineapple, mango, and lime slices. If time allows, cover and refrigerate for 2–4 hours, although you may serve it right away.

• Before serving, stir in the club soda. Fill large wine glasses with ice cubes. Ladle the sangria, with the fruit slices, into the glasses and serve.

sangria de cava

4 oz (120 ml) framboise (raspberry liqueur) • 1 oz (30 ml) fresh lemon juice • 2 tablespoons superfine sugar • ½ pound (250 g) ripe strawberries, stemmed and sliced • ½ pound (250 g) ripe raspberries or blackberries • ½ pound (250 g) ripe blueberries • 1 lemon, thinly sliced and seeded • 1½ cups (375 ml) cranberry juice cocktail • 1 (750-ml) bottle Cava (Spanish sparkling wine) or other sparkling wine

• In a large nonreactive pitcher or punch bowl, stir together the framboise, lemon juice, and sugar until the sugar dissolves. Stir in the strawberries, raspberries, blueberries, and lemon slices, then stir in the cranberry juice cocktail. Cover and refrigerate for 2–4 hours, stirring occasionally.

• Ladle the fruit mixture into glasses until about halfway full, making sure to include a mix of fruit in each glass. Add several ice cubes, then pour in the Cava to fill the glass. Serve immediately.

tequila sunrise

3 ounces (90 ml) white tequila • 6 ounces (180 ml) fresh orange juice • 2–3 teaspoons grenadine • 1 orange wedge, raw sugar, and grated orange zest, for coating rim (optional)

• Fill a tall highball or Collins glass with ice cubes. Pour in the tequila, then the orange juice. Drizzle in the grenadine to taste, allowing it to settle to the bottom of the glass, and serve.

• For a festive sugared rim, pour a layer of raw sugar and grated orange zest onto a plate that's larger than the glass rim. Moisten the rim with an orange wedge, then press it into the sugar mix.

POMEGRANATE-FLAVORED GRENADINE SYRUP SWIRLS DOWN INTO THE CLASSIC TEQUILA SUNRISE, EVOKING A MORNING SKY. PLANTER'S PUNCH IS A COOL FAVORITE THAT ORIGINATED WITH JAMAICAN PLANTERS.

planter's punch

2 oz (60 ml) dark rum • 2 oz (60 ml) pineapple juice • 1 oz (30 ml) grapefruit juice • 1 oz (30 ml) fresh lime juice • 1 tablespoon superfine sugar • 2 oz (60 ml) club soda • 1 fresh pineapple wedge, for garnish

• Fill a cocktail shaker about two-thirds full with ice cubes. Add the rum, pineapple juice, grapefruit juice, lime juice, and superfine sugar. Shake vigorously for 15–20 seconds.

• Fill a tall highball or Collins glass with ice cubes. Strain the cocktail mixture into the glass. Pour in the club soda to top off, and stir briefly with a bar spoon or swizzle stick. Garnish with the pineapple wedge and serve immediately.

mojito

THIS CUBAN CLASSIC IS SAID TO HAVE BEEN A FAVORITE OF ERNEST HEMINGWAY. IT HAS JUST THE RIGHT BALANCE OF MINT, LIME, RUM, AND SUGAR TO CHASE THIRST AWAY ON A SULTRY SUMMER'S DAY.

2 or 3 sugar cubes • ¼ cup (10 g) fresh mint leaves • 1½ tablespoons fresh lime juice • 2 oz (60 ml) light rum • 3 oz (90 ml) club soda • 1 lime wedge and 1 sprig fresh mint, for garnish

- In the bottom of a sturdy tall highball or pint glass, muddle the sugar cubes, mint leaves, and lime juice together with a muddler, pounding firmly but gently and grinding the ingredients together until the sugar cubes are crushed and partially dissolved.

- Fill the glass with ice cubes. Add the rum, then pour in the soda. Stir well with a bar spoon or swizzle stick. Garnish with the lime wedge and mint sprig and serve immediately.

- For an unusual, spicy version, try substituting fresh basil leaves for the mint, and lemon for the lime.

fresh frozen

- To make a blended version (left, opposite page) muddle the sugar, mint, and lime juice in a glass. Add the rum, and steep for two hours. Put a glassful of ice cubes into a blender; pour in the rum mixture through a fine-mesh sieve. Add another ¼ cup (10 g) of fresh mint leaves along with the club soda. Cover and blend until smooth.

sake mojito

2 sugar cubes • ¼ cup (10 g) fresh mint leaves • 1 oz (30 ml) fresh lime juice • 3 oz (90 ml) sake • 2 oz (60 ml) club soda • 1 lemon slice and fresh mint, for garnish

● Put the sugar cubes, mint leaves, and lime juice in the bottom of a sturdy highball glass. With a muddler, firmly but gently pound and grind the ingredients together until the sugar cubes are crushed and partially dissolved.

● Fill the glass with ice cubes. Add the sake, then pour in the soda. Stir well with a swizzle stick or bar spoon. Garnish with the lemon slice folded on a cocktail pick and the mint sprig, and serve.

make it special

● Add creative details geared toward the drinks you're serving. For the sake mojito, use origami paper to make coasters, or wrap the drinks in the paper and tie them with a bit of palm twine or raffia. A coco-limon mojito can be enhanced with the addition of a coconut rim: dip the rim of the glass in light corn syrup, then into a plate of shaved coconut.
● Like many spirits, rum is now available in a wide variety of flavors, making it easy to create new variations of the classic mojito. You can also experiment with additions of fresh fruit such as raspberries.

coco-limon mojito

1 or 2 sugar cubes • ¼ cup (10 g) fresh mint leaves • 1 tablespoon fresh lemon juice • 2 oz (60 ml) coconut-flavored rum • 3 oz (90 ml) lemon-flavored soda • 1 strip lemon zest, 3 inches (7.5 cm) long, for garnish

● In the bottom of a highball glass, combine the sugar cube(s), mint leaves, and lemon juice. Firmly but gently pound and grind the ingredients together with a muddler, until the sugar is crushed and partially dissolved.

● Fill the glass with ice. Add the coconut-flavored rum, then pour in the lemon soda. Stir well with a bar spoon or swizzle stick. Garnish with the lemon zest, skewered on a cocktail pick, and fresh mint.

ginger twilight mojito

2 or 3 sugar cubes • 1 slice fresh ginger, about ¼ inch (6 mm) thick and 1 inch (2.5 cm) in diameter • 1 tablespoon fresh lime juice • 2 oz (60 ml) spiced rum • 3 oz (90 ml) club soda • 2 slices crystallized ginger, for garnish

● Muddle the sugar cubes, fresh ginger, and lime juice in a highball or old-fashioned glass as with the previous mojitos.

● Fill the glass with ice cubes. Add the spiced rum, then pour in the soda. Stir well with a bar spoon or swizzle stick. Spear two slices of crystallized ginger on a cocktail pick and place it in the drink, resting it along the side of the glass.

champagne cocktail

THIS PARAGON OF SIMPLE ELEGANCE DATES TO THE MID-19TH CENTURY.
A BITTERS-SOAKED SUGAR CUBE AND A TWIST OF LEMON ZEST GIVE A
DIGNIFIED LIFT TO EVEN THE MOST HUMBLE SPARKLER.

1 sugar cube • 2 or 3 drops Angostura bitters • 5 oz (150 ml)
well-chilled champagne or sparkling wine • 1 strip lemon zest,
3 inches (7.5 cm) long, for garnish

● Place the sugar cube on a small plate and carefully drip the
bitters onto the cube. Put the sugar cube in a champagne flute.

● Slowly pour the champagne into the glass. Hold the lemon
zest strip over the glass, and twist it in opposite directions to
release its oils before dropping it into the glass.

● For added drama, pour the champagne into the flutes first.
Prepare the sugar cubes beforehand by dropping the bitters onto
them, and let each guest drop a cube into a glass before toasting.

a votre santé

● Make it easy for guests to
keep track of glasses by attaching
small initialed tags (available at
stationery stores) to the stems.
● Turn this cocktail into a version
of a "French 75": mix 1 oz (30 ml)
cognac with 1 tablespoon lemon
juice and add it to the flute
before adding the sugar cube.

kir framboise royale

4 oz (120 ml) well-chilled champagne or other sparkling wine • 1 tablespoon framboise (raspberry liqueur) • 1 tablespoon crème de cassis • fresh raspberries, for garnish

● Chill a champagne flute in the freezer. Pour in the champagne, then add the framboise and crème de cassis. Garnish with the raspberries.

champagne service

● Champagne should always be served in long-stemmed flutes or tulip-shaped glasses, which enhance the rise of bubbles to the crown and concentrate the aromas.

● Use caution when opening champagne and sparkling wines. It's wise to keep a finger or thumb on the cork as you undo the cage, to prevent the cork from bursting out.

● Though popping the cork may seem festive, it dissipates some of the bubbles and affects the wine's taste. The bottle should "sigh," not pop. Hold the cork and turn the bottle (rather than turning the cork), dislodging the cork as gently as you possibly can.

bellini bella

1½ oz (45 ml) well-chilled peach nectar • 1 teaspoon lemon juice • 1 tablespoon peach schnapps • 4 oz (120 ml) well-chilled prosecco or other sparkling wine • 1 thin wedge fresh peach, for garnish

● Chill a champagne flute in the freezer.

● In a small measuring cup, stir together the peach nectar, lemon juice, and peach schnapps.

● Just before serving, pour the peach nectar mixture into the chilled flute. Slowly pour in the prosecco. Stir gently with a swizzle stick or bar spoon, garnish with the peach wedge, and serve.

berry merry christmas

1 sugar cube • 2 drops orange or Angostura bitters • 4 oz (120 ml) well-chilled champagne or sparkling wine • 1 oz (30 ml) well-chilled cranberry juice cocktail • fresh or frozen cranberries, for garnish

● Chill a champagne flute in the freezer.

● Put the sugar cube on a small plate. Gently shake the drops of bitters onto the sugar cube.

● Pour the champagne into the chilled flute. Add the cranberry juice. Drop the sugar cube into the glass, garnish with a few cranberries, and serve.

BLACK RUSSIANS, BRANDY ALEXANDERS, CLASSIC FRENCH-STYLE

CRAVINGS FOR DECADENT rich indulgences

CAP OFF A MEMORABLE OCCASION
BY SERVING DRINKS THAT INVITE GUESTS
TO LINGER A LITTLE WHILE LONGER

"How about a nightcap?" That time-honored offer signals a congenial and cozy transition towards evening's end, and perfectly captures the way that drinks can conclude a party in soothing style.

Some people like to transform spirited liquids into a form of dessert, adding cream to vodka and coffee liqueur to make a white Russian (page 81), for example, or layering liqueurs with complementary flavors and colors to make a classic French-style pousse-café (page 85). Other recipes, by contrast, add spirits and spices to coffee to make intensely flavorful concoctions that are best appreciated in small, slow sips. Both approaches offer an ideal way to prolong the pleasures of good company, whether you're seated around the dinner table, on the terrace, in the living room, or beside the fireplace.

eggnog

THIS TRADITIONAL HOLIDAY TREAT CAN BE SERVED HOT OR COLD.
INSPIRED BY A POTTERY BARN FAMILY RECIPE, THIS OLD-FASHIONED
EGGNOG NICELY BALANCES RICHNESS, SWEETNESS, SPICE, AND SPIRITS.

6 eggs • ¾ cup (180 ml) sugar • 2 cups (500 ml) milk • 2 cups (500 ml) brandy • ⅔ cup (160 ml) Jamaican rum • ¼ cup (60 ml) Grand Marnier or Cointreau • 1 teaspoon vanilla extract • 2 cups (500 ml) heavy cream, chilled • freshly grated nutmeg, for garnish

● Put the eggs and sugar in a pot and whisk briefly until smooth. Put the pot over the lowest possible heat and whisk continuously, just until the eggs are warmed, 3–5 minutes, taking care not to let them curdle. Still whisking, add the milk, brandy, rum, Grand Marnier, vanilla, and half of the cream. Raise the heat slightly and cook, stirring frequently, until hot but not boiling, 8–10 minutes.

● Remove from the heat. Whisk in the remaining cream. Pour into a heatproof punch bowl. Serve warm, or cover and transfer to the refrigerator to chill. Before serving, lightly dust the surface with nutmeg; ladle into glass mugs, and dust with more nutmeg.

make merry

● To give your presentation a quiet elegance, place the punch bowl on a silver platter and arrange cut-glass ornaments around its base.

● Chocolatey peppermint bark extends the holiday theme.

● New heat-resistant double-walled glasses (opposite page) give hot drinks contemporary style and may be used with cold drinks as well.

black russian

2 oz (60 ml) vodka • 1–1½ oz (30–45 ml) coffee-flavored liqueur (such as Kahlúa or Tía Maria)

- Fill an old-fashioned glass with ice cubes. Pour in the vodka. Add coffee liqueur to taste, using less if you prefer a drier cocktail, more if you like it sweeter. Stir briefly with a bar spoon or swizzle stick. Serve immediately.

- For a variation on the classic, you might substitute other spirits for the vodka; using Irish whiskey instead yields a "black Irish"; a "blackjack" is made with Jack Daniels bourbon instead of vodka.

sweet inspiration

- Serve drinks on individual trays accompanied by chocolate-covered espresso beans.
- For a frappé-style black Russian, serve the drink over crushed ice instead of ice cubes, or blend it in a blender.

POPULAR SINCE THE 1960s, THE SOPHISTICATED "RUSSIANS" PAIR WELL WITH STRONG COFFEE. SUBSTITUTE DIFFERENT SPIRITS TO LEND ADDED INTRIGUE TO THESE CROWD-PLEASING CLASSIC DRINKS.

white russian

2 oz (60 ml) vodka • 1 oz (30 ml) coffee-flavored liqueur (such as Kahlúa or Tía Maria) • 1 oz (30 ml) heavy cream

- Fill an old-fashioned glass with ice cubes. Pour in the vodka, add the coffee liqueur, and stir briefly with a bar spoon or swizzle stick. Drizzle in the cream, shaking the glass slightly to swirl it in.

- For variations on the white Russian, add a splash of soda to temper the sweetness; substitute orange-flavored vodka for the plain vodka; substitute dark crème de cacao for the Kahlúa to create a "brown Russian"; or substitute Irish cream liqueur for the cream.

make mine vanilla

- Instead of a swizzle stick, use a vanilla bean to swirl the cream into the drink.
- For more vanilla flavor, substitute a vanilla-flavored vodka for the plain vodka in the drink recipe.

brandy alexander

SIP AFTER SIP, THIS LONGTIME AFTER-DINNER FAVORITE CAPTURES THE APPEAL OF A CREAMY CHOCOLATE TRUFFLE, WITH THE ADDED WARMTH OF BRANDY AND THE SILKY RICHNESS OF CRÈME DE CACAO.

sugar and spice

• To make chocolate shavings, draw a swivel-bladed vegetable peeler along the edge of a room-temperature chocolate bar

• For a "brandy Alejandro," substitute Mexican brandy and mix ground cinnamon with the cocoa powder for dusting.

• A set of glasses in a rainbow of different colors adds variety to pale-hued drinks – and helps guests identify which is theirs.

2 oz (60 ml) brandy • 1 oz (30 ml) dark crème de cacao • 1 oz (30 ml) heavy cream • cocoa powder and fresh chocolate shavings, for garnish

• Chill a martini or other cocktail glass in the freezer or by filling it with ice cubes and water and setting it aside to chill.

• Put the brandy, crème de cacao, and cream in a cocktail shaker two-thirds filled with ice cubes. Shake for 15–20 seconds.

• Remove the glass from the freezer or empty out the ice cubes and water, shaking out any drops. Strain the drink into the chilled glass. Sprinkle lightly with a little cocoa powder and some chocolate shavings to garnish, and serve. For a less sweet garnish, dust the top of the drink with a sprinkle of grated nutmeg.

• For an updated take on this classic, substitute vanilla-flavored vodka for the brandy and light crème de cacao for dark.

pousse-café

FRENCH FOR "COFFEE-PUSHER," THE POUSSE-CAFÉ HAS BEEN MAKING AFTER-DINNER COFFEE A PLEASURE SINCE THE MID-19TH CENTURY. CAREFUL LAYERING OF THE LIQUEURS GIVES THE BEST EFFECT.

1½ tablespoons grenadine, chilled • 1½ tablespoons green crème de menthe, chilled • 1½ tablespoons light rum, chilled

● Pour the grenadine into a pousse-café glass or other tall, narrow liqueur glass.

● Hold the back of a slender teaspoon with its tip just above the surface of the grenadine. Slowly trickle the crème de menthe down the back of the spoon so that it floats on top of the grenadine (see step-by-step photos on the following pages).

● Rinse the spoon, then, using the same technique, layer the light rum to float on top of the crème de menthe. Take care not to disturb the glass as you serve; it is meant to be sipped in layers.

● This recipe is easily adapted to use your favorite liqueurs, but always layer the liqueurs in order of their density.

custom options

● Create your own favorites by selecting other spirits or liqueurs with complementary flavors, such as crème de cassis, white crème de menthe, and blue curaçao, or Kahlúa, Irish cream, and Frangelico.

● Put the liqueurs you'll be using into the freezer for one hour before you're ready to serve them to thicken them slightly.

one Assemble the liquids for
the pousse-café. For easy pouring
and attractive tableside presentation,
prepare a clean bottle for each,
labeling it with a decorative tag.

two Insert a clean funnel into
the neck of a bottle. Pour the
liqueur from its container into the
funnel to fill the new bottle. Chill the
filled bottles before using.

three Insert a pouring spout with a narrow nozzle into the neck of each bottle. Place a pousse-café glass on an individual serving tray. Carefully pour in the first liquid.

four Hold the tip of a bar spoon close to but not touching the surface of the liquid. Drizzle the next liquid down the back of the spoon's bowl. Repeat with the final liqueur.

irish coffee

THIS AFTER-DINNER FAVORITE WAS FIRST SERVED AT IRELAND'S SHANNON AIRPORT IN THE 1940s AND QUICKLY CAUGHT ON, ESPECIALLY IN AMERICA. HIGH-QUALITY WHISKEY AND STRONG COFFEE ENSURE SUCCESS.

delicious style

- To add a touch of Ireland's favorite color, drizzle a little green crème de menthe over the whipped cream before serving.

- To make the presentation more special, brew a pot of strong coffee in a cafetière and present the cafetière, shot glasses or cordial glasses full of Irish whiskey, and a bowl of lightly whipped cream on a tray, and let guests make their own drinks.

2 oz (60 ml) Irish whiskey • 1–1½ teaspoons superfine sugar • 6 oz (180 ml) hot, strong freshly brewed coffee • 2 heaping tablespoons lightly whipped chilled heavy cream

- Heat an Irish-coffee mug, stemmed goblet, or snifter by pouring boiling water into it and setting it aside for a moment to heat, then emptying the water, shaking out any remaining drops.

- Put the whiskey, along with sugar to taste, in the mug, goblet, or snifter and stir with a bar spoon until the sugar dissolves.

- Pour in the coffee and stir briefly. Spoon the whipped cream on top and serve immediately. (Note: the cream should be whipped only until it just begins to thicken.)

- Traditionalists insist that you not stir the coffee after adding the cream. The coffee is meant to be sipped though the cream.

mocha brûlot royale

1 cup (250 ml) brandy • 1 tablespoon sugar • 6 whole cloves • 4 strips orange zest, 3 inches (7.5 cm) long, cut with a swivel-bladed vegetable peeler • 2 cinnamon sticks, broken in half • 2 oz (60 ml) dark crème de cacao • 3 cups (750 ml) strong black freshly brewed coffee • 4 oz (120 ml) lightly whipped heavy cream • cinnamon sticks and shaved chocolate, for garnish

● Combine the brandy, sugar, cloves, orange zest, and cinnamon sticks in a nonreactive saucepan. Heat over medium-high heat, stirring occasionally, just until the mixture begins to simmer. Remove the pan from the heat to an open area on the kitchen counter or near the sink.

● Strike a long wooden match and slowly and very carefully bring the flame near the surface of the liquid to ignite the brandy's fumes. Let the brandy flame for about 30 seconds. Then, cover the pan to extinguish the flames. Uncover and stir in the crème de cacao. Ladle the mixture into 4 glasses or mugs. Add the coffee and top with whipped cream. Garnish with cinnamon sticks and sprinkles of freshly shaved chocolate. Serves 4.

cafe à la russe

2 oz (60 ml) vodka • 2 oz (60 ml) freshly brewed espresso-strength coffee • 1–1½ teaspoons superfine sugar • 1 tablespoon heavy cream • 3 chocolate-covered coffee beans and ground cinnamon, for garnish

● Fill a cocktail shaker two-thirds full with ice cubes. Add the vodka, coffee, sugar to taste, and cream. Shake vigorously for 15–20 seconds.

● Fill a tall old-fashioned or pint glass with ice cubes. Strain the drink into the glass. Garnish the froth on top with the chocolate-covered espresso beans and a dusting of cinnamon, and serve.

jamaican coffee frappé

2 oz (60 ml) dark spiced rum • 1–1½ teaspoons superfine sugar • 6 oz (180 ml) strong black coffee, preferably Jamaican Blue Mountain, cooled • 1 oz (30 ml) chilled heavy cream • 1 cup (250 ml) ice cubes

● Put the rum, sugar, coffee, cream, and ice cubes into the jar of a bar blender. Cover and blend until well mixed and smooth, about 30 seconds. Pour into a chilled glass, and garnish with a little whipped cream, if desired.

wrap it up

● You can easily create drink "cozies" like the ones shown here, to make hot or cold drinks more comfortable to hold. Simply cut squares of felt about 6 x 6 inches (15 x 15 cm). Place a glass on top of each fabric square, lift up the corners, and tie each glass with a thin leather lace. Tie beads to the ends of the laces.

GLOSSARY

Aperitif A term for any spirit-based drink sipped before dining with the purpose of stimulating the appetite.

Bar spoon A long, slender spoon used to stir cocktails and other mixed drinks.

Beer This popular beverage is made by fermenting mashed cooked grains and hops. Lager-style beers are the familiar pale golden beers popular in America.

Bitters Distilled from secret formulas of botanical ingredients, these highly concentrated alcoholic elixirs – of which the most familiar brands are Angostura and Peychaud – are used just a few drops at a time to add a hint of flavor to mixed drinks.

Boston shaker A type of cocktail shaker consisting of one tall, sturdy glass with straight, sloping sides and a similar metal container that is inverted snugly over it, forming a tight seal while liquid ingredients and ice are agitated. Those drinks that are stirred rather than shaken may be mixed with a bar spoon in the glass portion.

Bourbon From Kentucky and other parts of the American South, this type of whiskey is distilled from a mash of fermented grains and must contain at least 51 percent corn, combined with malted barley and rye or wheat, producing a full-bodied flavor.

Brandy Any strong spirit distilled from fermented fruit juice, of which the most common source is wine made from grapes. Other brandies may be made from such fruits as peaches, raspberries, cherries, or apples; but when the term "brandy" is used alone, it refers always to grape brandy.

Cava A term referring to the sparkling wine produced primarily in northeastern Spain, made from a blend of seven grapes, including Chardonnay and Pinot Noir, that gives it a rich, fruity, yet dry character.

Champagne Although this term is misused to refer to any sparkling wine, it specifically designates those carefully produced, complex sparkling wines made according to tradition (and law) in the northeastern French region of the same name.

Cocktail Any mixed drink that is shaken or stirred and then poured or strained into a cocktail glass.

Cocktail shaker Any of a variety of sturdy watertight containers used to mix drink ingredients while quickly chilling them with ice cubes. While the Boston shaker variety is made up of two glasses, those referred to as "cocktail shakers" generally are composed of a glass or metal beaker atop which sits a snug metal top with a built-in strainer covered with a cap.

Coffee-flavored liqueur Coffee beans or brewed coffee is featured as the flavoring ingredient in a wide range of popular sweet liqueurs such as Kahlúa and Tía Maria.

Cognac A type of well-aged wine-based brandy produced in the Cognac region of southwestern France, prized for its purity and mellowness of flavor.

Cordial A sweet alcoholic beverage, also generally referred to as a liqueur, based on a spirit, a sweetener, and one or more complementary flavorings. See also "Liqueur."

Curaçao Originally made with fruit from the Caribbean island of the same name (still used in some premium brands), this liqueur is intensely flavored with the essence of orange peel. It is available in a clear colorless "white" version as well as in colored forms, including orange, green, brown, and blue.

Dash A drink ingredient measurement equivalent to $\frac{1}{8}$ teaspoon, named for the rapid wrist motion used to dispense such bottled flavoring agents as bitters, hot pepper sauce, or Worcestershire sauce.

Digestif Refers to beverages, often spirit-based, sipped after a meal to aid the digestive process.

Garnish Any fruit or vegetable – including sweet maraschino or fresh cherries, orange slices or wedges, whole strawberries, mint sprigs, celery stalks, and pickled olives or cocktail onions – added to a drink just before serving, not only to enhance its visual appeal, but also sometimes to provide a pleasurable nibble.

Gin A clear spirit distilled from a grain mash, flavored with botanical ingredients that always include juniper berries, which give it a clean, bracing flavor.

Grenadine A deep blush-colored syrup for coloring and flavoring drinks, sometimes made with pomegranate juice.

Hawthorn strainer A kind of strainer for shaken or stirred drinks, characterized by a flat, circular piece of screen with a metal spring coil around its rim that holds it snugly in place over a mixing glass.

Highball A simple mixed drink that usually consists of just two ingredients, a spirit and a mixer, poured directly into a tall highball glass filled with ice.

Hot pepper sauce Any of a wide variety of different commercially bottled condiments made from hot red chili peppers, of which the most widely known brand is Tabasco.

Jigger A liquid measurement equivalent to 1½ ounces (45 ml), as well as a small vessel used to measure that amount when mixing drinks.

Lager See beer, lager-style.

Lillet A French brand of aperitif made from Bordeaux wine fortified with Armagnac and a proprietary blend of herbs, spices, and fruits. Lillet is available in *blanc* (white) and *rouge* (red), each with its own flavors.

Lime juice, bottled sweetened A popular source of citrusy tang and sweetness for mixed drinks. The most commonly available brand is Rose's.

Limoncello An Italian digestif produced along the Amalfi Coast, made by steeping lemon peels in clear spirits, sweetening with sugar, and diluting with water.

Liqueur Also referred to as a cordial, this sweetened spirit may be flavored with fruits, nuts, herbs, spices, or other botanical essences, either singly or in combination, to produce an intensely flavored liquid that may be sipped on its own as an after-dinner drink or used to flavor mixed drinks

Maraschino cherry Frequently used as a garnish for drinks, often with its stem still attached, this bottled pitted red cherry has been steeped in and dyed in a flavored sugar syrup. Red maraschino cherries are slightly flavored with almond, green ones with mint.

Melon liqueur A bright neon-green liqueur flavored with honeydew melon, most commonly known by the Japanese brand name Midori.

Mixed drink Any drink made with two or more liquid ingredients, at least one of which includes alcohol. The cocktail and the highball are the two most common subcategories.

Mixer Any nonalcoholic liquid that is combined with an alcoholic liquid to make a mixed drink. Included in this category are sodas such as cola, lemon-lime soda, ginger ale, and flavorless club soda; fruit juices; and tomato juice.

Mixing glass The tall, sloping-sided glass portion of a Boston shaker.

Muddling The process of mashing together sugar cubes or granulated sugar with aromatic or flavorful ingredients such as fresh mint, fruit, or bitters to combine and release their flavors before ice and liquids are added. The long, narrow pestle known as a "muddler" is the most convenient tool for the job, although the back of a sturdy spoon may also be used.

Orange-flavored liqueur Orange is a very popular liqueur flavor, with numerous brands available and sometimes referred to categorically by the term "triple sec" or Curaçao. Two of the most popular brands of orange-flavored liqueur are Cointreau and Grand Marnier, both of which have been produced in France since the 19th century.

Orgeat A sweet, thick, milky-hued syrup made with almonds and either rose water or orange-flower water, used to flavor and sweeten mixed drinks. If you can't find orgeat, substitute one of the clear bottled almond-flavored syrups now widely available for flavoring coffee.

Prosecco An aromatic, fruity, light sparkling wine produced in northeastern Italy from a grape variety of the same name.

Rum A spirit of the Caribbean and South America, distilled from molasses or sugar-cane juice. White or light rum has been filtered to remove all traces of color. Golden and dark rums may get their colors and

additional flavor from the omission of that final filtration, from aging in oak casks, or from the addition of caramel. Many distillers now also market flavored rums.

Rye A type of whiskey made from a fermented grain mash that includes at least 51 percent rye grains, generally aged in new charred oak barrels.

Sake A Japanese wine, generally dry, made from rice and water, with a mellow flavor and lingering sweetness. Traditionally sipped cool or warm, sake has also found favor as a mixed drink ingredient.

Schnapps A German term that technically refers to a clear brandy or eau-de-vie based on fruit or some other botanical ingredient. The word "schnapps" is also used to refer to a commercially bottled sweetened brandy similar to a liqueur, such as peppermint or peach schnapps.

Scotch Another term for whisky produced in Scotland. Among the most popular Scotches are "single-malt" varieties, made by individual distilleries from their own malted barley mashes then aged in oak barrels for three years (or many more) before finally being bottled without blending. Single-malt Scotch should be savored on its own, never used as part of a mixed drink.

Shot A single, neat portion of a spirit, equivalent to 1½ oz (45 ml), generally measured in a measuring glass of the same name. Note, however, that not all glasses sold as shot glasses may be precise, and some hold as much as 2 oz (60 ml).

Southern Comfort A brand of fruit-flavored liqueur made by steeping peaches and other ingredients in a base of Bourbon.

Sparkling wine A generic term referring to any wine that contains small bubbles of carbon dioxide gas. Usually, this is produced by a secondary fermentation of the wine that occurs within the bottle, a process referred to as "méthode champenoise," a reference to the classic method developed in the Champagne region of France.

Sugar, superfine, A form of white sugar, widely available in food stores, that has been finely ground to help it dissolve quickly and thoroughly in liquids, making it a convenient way to sweeten mixed drinks.

Swizzle stick A slender rod that may be used either to mix a drink in a pitcher or glass before serving or to stir it between sips. Swizzle sticks may range from fanciful disposable plastic varieties to reusable glass or metal sticks of various decorative designs.

Tequila A liquor made in the Tequila region of Mexico, fermented and distilled from the steam-roasted and mashed hearts of the blue agave plant. Tequila *blanco*, known in English as "white" or "silver" tequila, is a sparkling-clear unaged spirit with a bright, slightly peppery flavor. Gold tequila contains a percentage of two-month-old aged tequila and may also include caramel or other flavoring agents to enhance its smoothness. Tequila *reposado*, literally "rested," has been aged in oak for a minimum of two months, yielding a smoother, rounder flavor. Tequila *añejo*, or "aged," has spent at least one year (and often many more) in oak barrels, giving it a dark color and a rich, round flavor.

Vermouth A white wine that has been slightly fortified with additional alcohol and given subtle aromas from blends of botanical ingredients. Available in both dry and sweet forms, vermouth is most often used in small amounts as a modifier for drinks based on other spirits.

Vodka A clear, relatively flavorless spirit distilled from a fermented mash of grains or vegetables such as potatoes. Look also for a wide range of vodkas now available flavored with essences of fruits and spices.

Whisk(e)y A spirit distilled from a fermented mash of grains and aged in wooden casks, resulting in an amber color and a rich, round flavor. The spelling "whisky" refers specifically to those products made and bottled in either Scotland or Canada, while "whiskey" designates those produced in Ireland or the United States.

Zest The outermost, brightly colored layer of a citrus fruit's peel, full of flavorful essential oils. When a recipe calls for zest, remove it with a special zesting tool, a sharp paring knife, or a swivel-bladed vegetable peeler, taking care to leave behind the spongy, bitter-tasting layer of pith beneath it.

INDEX

ACKNOWLEDGMENTS

Author Norman Kolpas would like to thank Katie and Jake for their support during the production of this book.

Weldon Owen would like to thank the photography and editorial teams, and acknowledge the following people and organizations:

Copy Editor
Sharron Wood

Indexer
Ken DellaPenta

Associate Stylist
Elisabet der Nederlanden

Photography Assistant
Tom Hood

Lead Merchandise Coordinator
Mario Serafin

Merchandise Coordinator
Peter Jewett

Assistance, advice, or support
Birdman, Inc., Sarah Putman Clegg, Elizabeth Dougherty, the Griggs family, Kass Kapsiak (Catering by Kass), Charlie Path, Sara Terrien, and the Pottery Barn product development team and staff at the Pottery Barn Store, Corte Madera, California.